S0-AEM-544

DREAM
CANTOS:
To Get a Life

BY

Charles W.T. Stephenson

By the same author:

Development Cantos (1993)

© Copyright 2001 Charles W.T. Stephenson
All rights reserved.
Torquilstone Press
3106 Cathedral Avenue N.W.
Washington, D.C. 20008-3419
202-338-4086

International Standard Book Number: 0-9638907-3-5

For
Will
and
Maimie

CANTOS

STARTING POINTS

WILL AND MAIMIE

CONVERGENCES

A TIME, NOT FAR AWAY

SCHOOLS

TESTS

WAR

PEACE

PERCEPTIONS

CONCEPTUAL BRIDGES

COMMUNICATION

CONCLUSIONS

Preface

I use the word "dream" in this book in the sense of "aspirations," not in the sense of thoughts occurring in sleep, although the latter may also illuminate our lives.

A canto is a sub-division of a longer poem.

My first book, entitled "Development Cantos," drew on my experience as a lawyer for the U.S. Agency for International Development (USAID), and suggested that the development of a country can be compared to the development of a person.

This volume asks, accordingly, how do you promote the development of a person — of oneself, or of someone else? In the vernacular, how do you help a person get a life?

My father, William Stephenson, had concrete ideas on this subject. So has my mother, Maimie. So do I.

My father's background, in physics and psychology, made him say that he hoped the insights of psychology would pave the world's way to peace, before the insights of physics blew it up.

My mother's background has been art: the joy, as she describes it, of creating something, and preserving it, so that others may have joy of it, too. Her illustrations adorn "Development Cantos" and this book.

Author's Note

I am sometimes asked how I came to write these Cantos. The process began with a USAID paper on "The Role of Imagination in Providing Legal Services for Development," in 1979. Other papers on development followed.

Papers I have written over the years for meetings of the Policy Sciences Center of New Haven, Connecticut, are reflected here, also. The Center carries on the work of Professors Myres S. McDougal and Harold D. Lasswell, my favorite teachers at Yale Law School.

I don't compare my work to the famous Cantos of Ezra Pound, but I am most grateful for a minor geographical linkage. Thanks to the great kindness of Mary de Rachewiltz, Ezra Pound's daughter, and her husband, Boris, I started the final draft of "Development Cantos" on the uppermost turret of their castle in Northern Italy.

Acknowledgements

If I could list everyone who has been helpful, the list would be very long.

Highlights would be:

My parents.

My father's colleagues and students, especially two of his Ph.D. students: Professor Joye Patterson Nunn of the Journalism School of the University of Missouri at Columbia, and Professor Steven R. Brown of the Political Science Department of Kent State University, Ohio.

The Washington D.C. Area Biography Group, led by Marc Pachter of the Smithsonian Institution, and the Group's members over time, especially Judith Grummon Nelson, Philip Kopper, and Pat McNees.

All others not here mentioned.

For her patience, support, and suggestions, my wife, Cathya.

The Stephenson Family   Oxford, Spring 1948
From left: Maimie, Mariel, Charles, Will, Richard and Averil

Wave!

STARTING POINTS

1. <u>Dreams</u>

These Cantos sing
of people's dreams - -
- - their aspirations - -
what they want from life.

The facts of the future
are built on dreams.

Dreams permit change
to happen.

Watch.

2. Start

"Start"
said Myres Smith McDougal
of Yale Law School,
that smithy of ideas
"with a clear definition
of the problem."

The problem is
to allow the future
to be better than the past

and to assure
that there will be a future.

This was my father's dream
for his children's lives
and for the lives of children everywhere.

His odyssey

and mine

and all of ours.

3. Maps of the Future

> A dream
> is a map
> of the future.

My father
William Stephenson
        known as "Will"

had dreams as ordinary
        as any father's wishes for his family

and dreams as wide
        as all mankind.

He died, too soon, in 1989,
leaving a world-wide web of friends and students
and a luminous legacy:

> a way of making maps of thought
> to help us understand ourselves
> - - what we think now,
> and what we dream - -

> like a tool kit

> to help fix
> the flat tires of the future.

3

4. Epicenters

Thought is like
a carousel:
fancy takes us
up and down
and round and round.

The epicenter of an earthquake
is the place on the surface of the globe
above the deeper center
where growls and shudders
record the release of tension underground.

Cold-war tensions in the world
are in repentance
but the epicenter
of the upward struggle
of the human race
to live its life in freedom

is still the landscape
where ideas of individuals
cooperate or conflict:
where people put thought into action
or refrain.

Harm in the world
is mostly caused
by what people do
or don't.

Therein lies the possibility for improvement:

people can learn:
understanding can advance.

4

Will's legacy was his method
to map such understanding,
to make it easier to perceive,
communicate, and cooperate,
adult to adult, parent to child.

"It doesn't matter
what you call a program"
Hubert Humphrey said,
crafting legislation,
"as long as you get 'mutual'
or 'cooperation' into the title."

Will's vision was upstream
from Humphrey's quip.

Will said
get understanding
of people's feelings
into the program first.

His method is known
as "Q,"
as in P, Q, R.

5. Gifts of Providence

"Just do the best
you can" was what
Will said.

But he would quietly
help you,
if he could.

These Cantos suggest
how to turn your dreams
for life

     into reality,
     if you can.

     And you can.

The short answer is
dream high
dream hard
accept support from friends

     and from those you do not know
     so that unplanned events
     will seem like positive gifts of Providence

and,
as much as you can,
try to get everything right

     within the time available
     for the task.

6. <u>Connections</u>

Our lives,
like music
from a carousel,
flow up and down
in rows of notes.

Children play a game
connecting up the numbered dots
upon a page:

a picture of a clown appears
as if by magic.

Adults go through life
connecting up the dots
of their experience

which are not numbered.

Choices must be made
of what connects with what.
A sure connection
we call logical.

Less sure,
we label fanciful.

If barely visible,
we call the seer
either a genius
or out of his mind.

Not all the dots of life connect, at first:

- - adjust the view - -

art is an infinite set of adjustments,
we are told.

The battleship
received a signal
to change course - -
"Do you know to
whom you are talking?"
its Admiral said - -
"this is a battleship!"

"Please
change course"
the signal came again - -
"this is a lighthouse."

Dreams are future connections
more likely to come true
if treated like any other idea in life:

capable of being promoted
and put into effect.

8

7. <u>Particles of Thought</u>

                    Will had a theory
                    - - more than a theory.
                    He knew.

People use words
to express the meanings of ideas.

Language deals with particles of thought
as physics deals with particles of matter.

                    Will, with his two Ph.D.'s,
                    in physics and psychology,
                    knew about both.

You can treat both kinds of particles alike,
he found (the statistics are the same)

          and introduce
          objective operations
          into the realm of thought
          into the realm of dreams:

                    make dreams hard
                    make them live
                    make them now.

8. Gentle Breakage

Break gently
to the human race

the thought

that there is no longer need
for warfare

all our energies
can go
for the survival of the planet

as a place of beauty.

From "Madonna and St. Anne"
of Leonardo da Vinci.

WILL AND MAIMIE

9. <u>Starting Small</u>

> Most carousels
> start slowly
> so as not to alarm
> the children
> or the parents.
> Life is like that.

It is important to remember
that people who do big things

    often start small

      with just themselves.

Will started small, himself,

the eldest of five children
in a coal-mining family
in the North of England.

His father was an engineer,
lamed in an accident down the pit,
at the local mine in Chopwell, County Durham.

    The roof of a tunnel had fallen:

everyone went down,
as was the custom,
to rescue those alive.

A second roof fall

trapped Will's father for a while
and hurt his hip and spine.

He was assigned
to tend the lamps the miners used

- - like Aladdin's helper - -

devising also useful things about the mine
and practicing mental arithmetic,
his hobby.

The house where Will grew up
was number-literate,

in a word.

10. <u>Home</u>

When Will was born
the 20th century
was two years old.

His parents
dreamed
for their children

as all parents do.

He dreamed
for his children
and for all children
everywhere.

When he was born,
England housed many of its workers
in identical row houses
side
     by
       side
touching one another

      kitchen and parlour down,
      bedrooms up, alley behind.

      Will's family lived in such a house
      when he was born.

"No plaque on the door yet!"
    said Aunt Erda,
    always cheerful,
    showing me the street
    Will's home was on,
    sloping down the hill toward the extinct mine.

    She was not sure
    which door was theirs
    but the sight moved me:

    perhaps it was the signature
    of poverty and pride

    and the memory of the mine
    with its slag heap behind it:

        an artificial mountain
        of rock and earth
        dug up to reach the coal,
        covered now
        with trees and grass.

            "I am the grass"
            said Walt Whitman.

            We all are,
            I believe.

11. <u>Whoopee!</u>

> Dreams
> are images
> which we later clothe
> with words.

Will's family
valued words
as well as numbers.

We children had holidays with his parents:
the Stephenson home by then was larger,
on the end of a different row of houses,
along the Roman Road to Ebchester

> where Grandfather would be buried
> by the church with the Saxon window.

I spent hours lying on the floor
with their illustrated encyclopedia
learning of exotic things

> like printing presses
> and pineapple plantations
> > pictured in orange
> > and sepia engravings.

Then, too, there was
a dictionary of anthropology,
illustrating the creations
> of simpler tribes
> than ours:

assagais,
knobkerries,
peace-pipes,
boomerangs,
and the like.

When the time has come
to integrate religions
let us allow
the usefulness of illustrations
to give access to ideas

        like the stained glass windows
        in Sainte Chapelle in Paris

        they called it Sainte Chapelle
        because it was a chapel.

I startled a busload of passengers once
by hollering "Whoopee"
as we got off the bus at Grandma's
for our holiday

      coming from Newcastle
      (new in 1172)
      where the train from Oxford
      had dropped us off.

           I do not think
           that I have ever
           before or since
           so publicly
           shared my joy
           with the world
           except perhaps
           when I got married.

12. Riddles

Will knew
that there is something
about happy holidays
when growing up
that lets a child
think well
of the rest of the world
for the rest
of its life.

We had excursions
on our holidays in the North.

There were no carousels,
but Hadrian's Wall was near;

so were Roman camps
with names like Corstopitum.

(As I tried to recall
the name of Corstopitum
there came to mind
Will's favorite riddle:
"What is the difference"
he asked
"between a riddle
and an elephant
sitting on a bun?"

"One is a conundrum,"
was the answer
"and the other
has a bun under um.")

I used to marvel
as I fell asleep at Grandma's
in the summer nights
that cars along the Roman road

        would cast
        a ray of light
        through my window
        and upon my ceiling

                which would travel
                in the opposite direction
                from the way
                the car was going.

Grandma's was a classic place for children:
across the road and down through the trees
was the Derwent River,
lazy in its flat, worn rocks

        ideal for hopping on.

Beyond the alley was a tiny shop
selling orange pop
("soda" to Americans)
and potato crisps
("chips" to Americans)
and other things

- - but what else mattered
to a child?

Under the roof behind the house

lay treasures for the eye:
a giant copper basin,
set in stone,
where the wash was done
and a mangle
with a handle we could turn
to press out water
from the clothes.

Inside, indeed,
the legendary kettle
warmed on the hob.

13. Luck

"Luck be a lady
tonight!"

- "Guys & Dolls."

We dream of luck
but work to do without it.

Luck is partly
individuals you find
who help you.

Will had luck: he found a teacher

who saw his brightness
and let him forage forward

rather than stay completely
in his class.

He foraged
for a B.A., M.A.,
and a Ph.D. in physics
out of Durham.

As it happened,
the year he got that Ph.D. from Durham
there were no jobs in England
for Ph.D.'s in physics - -
         the depression had arrived.
He got a fellowship, instead,
for a Ph.D. in London in psychology.

The fields were then
not so far apart:
      physics included the study of light, for instance;
      psychology, how the eye received it.

In fact, he went on learning all his life:
in teaching, in research, or with advertising firms
and as a consultant;
moving from time to time.

      When I was two
      he moved to Oxford University's
      Institute
      of Experimental Psychology.

He helped to found
the British Society for Psychical Research,
and was early in the Society for Research on Ageing.

In World War II, he helped the Royal Air Force,
and as a Brigadier, the British Army.
After the war, off to the psychology department
at the University of Chicago,
and visiting, at other universities.
Next, in Connecticut - near New York -
he worked in the private sector
      - - advertising
         and motivation research - -
with Nowland & Co., which leased the Luce estate
in Greenwich.

As the last arrival, his office was, he said,
Clare Booth Luce's palatial bathroom.

For the last 30 years of his life,
he was Distinguished Research Professor
at the University of Missouri's
Journalism School.

In ups and downs,
he said, he never
had something happen to him,
that he didn't find how
to turn to his advantage.

His odyssey
is working still
wide and deep.

"Life is a stairway to paradise, with a new step every day."

- - "An American in Paris."

Mohammed
fond of paradise
would approve.

Tongue in cheek, I say
that life
is a series
of silver linings

with moments
of pure gold
along the way.

14. <u>Patience</u>

"Wait until
you've seen Maimie"
Ernie McTaggart
told Will.

How do children find their dreams?

Dreams for children
start with parents.

Will and Maimie found each other
        meeting over tennis:
        she filled in as a fourth.
        She remembers his orange hair
        darting around across the net
        above his tennis whites.

Mary Brynhilde Richardson,
born when the century was four years old
found, when very young,
that "Mary" was hard to say
and came out "Maimie;"
the name has stuck
        for 97 years.

Her roots went deep
in Northern England - -

        her grandmother, Isabel Cosser,
        got her name from Sieur de Kossa

who came with other Norman knights
from France - -

                         undocumented aliens,
                         the Saxons called them.

De Kossa settled in Berwick - on - Tweed
        precisely on the English side
        of what is now the Scottish border.

                         People in our family
                         are often to be found
                         near a border
                         preserving the proximity
                         of an alternate dream.

        We do not know
        if Duke William, trusting him,
        wanted a good man
        on the Northern marches or whether,

        not taking avoidable chances
        de Kossa waited until the South of England
        was safely won,
        but then had to settle
        for land in the less popular North.

        Probably the conservative explanation should prevail,
        because the family stayed in Berwick
        for the next 800 years.

We are perversely proud
to have Bishop Ridley in Maimie's family - -
burned at the stake
in 1555 by Henry VIII.

The charge was heresy
but the motive was divorce.

        You tipped the executioner
                to use dry wood
                        for it to be over sooner.

An early photograph
shows the youthful Maimie
as slim, alive, bright of eye,
sparkling like a Celtic elf.

Her father, headmaster of a school,
had his children taught at home,
in the primary grades, in Newcastle.

        When the influenza epidemic,
                (spread, partly, by returning soldiers
                from the Great War
                - - flu killed a hundred million people, they say
                around the world)
        made it prudent to leave the city
        he moved them
        to their cottage
        at the edge of the moor
        a cottage of stone and slate

                standing, still,
                where the heather begins
                on the edge of the moor.

                      Always on the edge.

                        "If you're not on the edge"
                        said a T-shirt at my college
                        "you're wasting space."

Maimie.

Convergences.

CONVERGENCES

15. <u>Art is Long</u>

Maimie's family
have painted and etched the North of England
for generations back:
Uncle Ridley, Grandfather William,
the Thomas Miles Richardsons, Junior and Senior.

Maimie has always been an artist
in everything she touches.
George Bernard Shaw,
visiting a friend where Maimie lived,
called her "the little girl who paints."

        She could paint
        the angels down from Heaven
        and draw the devils
        back from Hell

        and have them reconciled
        in half an hour
        with the magic
        in her voice
        and her quiet logic.

      Part of the logic and the magic is the secret
      that she shared with Will:

        permit yourself to cross the border
        to where others sit:
        your view will benefit.

She could calm an angry crowd.

Students in Columbia, Missouri,

protesting Vietnam,
would not let the journalist
Harry Reasoner
reason with them.
"Let him speak
for common courtesy," she said.

"Little old lady for President,"
the crowd,
consenting,
cried.

She taught us children much:

Averil   1933 -
Charles 1935 -
Mariel   1939 -
Richard 1946 -

Part of Maimie's magic is
she does not seem to teach.

Things are around
which you happen to learn from
by yourself

except in art
where lessons are gentle and detailed
and tailored to her audience's speed.

Apart, perhaps, from Will's, and Arthur Liman's,
I've not been close
to a finer mind

> and in the nuances
> of telling good from ill
> without imposing
> she clearly exceeds us all.

> If women ran the world
> said my wife
> our small blue planet
> would be better off.

> Will said so too.

16. Muggleswick

> No, not
> "Muddleswick."

Maimie's cottage
at the edge of the moor
was at Muggleswick

> - - a Saxon name:
>> the wic or settlement
>> of Moclings,
>> the children or
>> descendants of Mocla.

>> So often,
>> things are named
>> for people,
>> like Parkinson's disease,
>> and Alzheimer's
>> named for the doctors
>> who first wrote them up.

Will and the McTaggart boys
took a camping holiday
near Maimie's cottage by the moor.

When the young men's supplies ran low
Maimie brought a pail of milk
each day across the field.

> ("Drink a pail of milk a day!")

Maimie and Will were married
in Muggleswick church
on Christmas Day of 1929.

                              The moor, with its
                              sheep,
                              lay behind the church
                              and lies there still.

The dairy farm,
stone and slate
lay downhill from the church

                    and lies there still

                    on the border,
                    always on the border.

From the farm
had come the milk
for the young men in their camp

            where they had lain
            not as soldiers getting ready
            for war
            but as dreamers
            getting ready to dream.

33

My roots
go into Muggleswick too
the heather
and the forget-me-nots
along the rivulet
where we played

- - water play is the best play - -

as children
near the edge
of the moor.

Visiting the church
as a young man from America
I put a pound in the poor box.

"A pound!" My grandmother
was scandalized
at my extravagance.

17. Legends and Life

Sometimes there are convergences in our lives:
things grow to be what we name them
and we name them from what they are.

These convergences
are defining moments of life.

The defining can last a lifetime
or be over soon
as the dream adjusts to reality
and reality to the dream.

Legends mark places
where dreams and reality
intersected in the past.

Maimie's parents
gave their children
names from the Norse legends:

Mary Brynhilde Richardson - Maimie -
who was awakened
by a man who knew no fear
from her ring of magic fire
and married him.

Her sister Isabel Erda - -
    Goddess of Wisdom
    in Old Norse
    teacher, painter, and friend to all
    who lives on the Great North
    - - no, not Norse - - Road
    from Newcastle.

Her brother William Siegfried Richardson
    amateur boxer, teacher, union organizer, and
    a Time - Lord (well, a chronometer-maker,
    where, in
    the final exam for the license,
    they give you a bar of mild steel
    and say: "Make a chronometer,
    please.")

It is told
that the Dalai Lama
approached a hot dog
vendor and said:
"Make me One
with Everything,
please."

Prairie Rose.

A TIME, NOT FAR AWAY

18. <u>Sustainable Beauty</u>

Accept the rose
as a symbol of beauty
for each life.

Will and Maimie's
relationship was roses.

Magnify
the symbol of a rose.

Let it become
the symbol
of a world-wide need for beauty

sustainable beauty
for a small blue planet.

19. Durable Challenges

There will come a time
not far away

when the tasks
of feeding, housing,
teaching, and keeping well the world

will be achieved.

We have the know-how
and the capacity
to do it now:

the problem is not the production
but the distribution.

After the basic needs of life are met
the challenge becomes
how to avoid
too many people unemployed.

Beauty is the answer:
making and preserving beauty.

In artifacts,
but also in planetary terms:
preserving the beauty
of the earth:
the plants and animals;

beautiful spaces;
our protective ozone;
the ecology of our environment.

It is a challenge:
humans increase
by 200,000 per day
though our acceleration
has begun to slow.

They say
man's challenge
should exceed his grasp

- - or what's a heaven for - -

but this challenge
is a do-able concern

not just a dream
not just a dream

Will thought
and I believe.

These are our children's challenges

as well as ours

their odyssey too.

20. Post-Natal Drip

Nature or nurture?

Speaking of children
it has been debated
how much of their life's accomplishments
come from the genes they inherit
and how much from what they learn.

Will had no doubt.

"Clearly"
          he wrote

"I am one of those
who hold that even though the child
has been formed

partly by heredity
and partly by environment,

the former
is but a spark
to the conflagration
that constitutes
the latter."

Get the best - -
and get it for everyone - -
was his philosophy.
Do not assume
that our capacities
are determined
at our birth

        he said

        pour on the fuel
        for fame.

Help the poorest in society
and the world.

        The humane view
        is also the most productive:

            what a child is given
            in life is far more important

            than the brains
            or caste
            of its parents.

21. <u>Coo</u>

What would you do, gentle reader,
knowing what you know now,
to temper the mild steel
your child is born as?

        The first ingredient
        for a child's success
        surely is pure love.

           You coo, or croon,
           dandle and chuckle with
           and watch the gentle
           rise and fall of sleep.

You guard the stairs
when they begin to crawl;
hold a finger out for them
when they begin to walk.

              Accept what help
              you find in life
              as every person must.

              Tell them stories
              even before
              they start to talk.

22. The Tortoise and Porpoise at Corpus

Will's Oxford
College,
Corpus Christi,
had in its
quadrangle
a fountain
where sported
and spouted
the statues
of a tortoise
and porpoise.

They stayed immobile
by day
but at night

in the bedtime tales Will told us

the tortoise would perambulate
about the college

returning before dawn
to the porpoise in the fountain
with tales of his moonlight adventures
and with snacks.

The dons, the next morning,
would be mystified
at who had moved
their books or telescopes
or who had pinched
their bread and cheese.

And so to bed
as Pepys
in his diaries
said.

Maimie

Show-off!

SCHOOLS

23. Choices

As any parent would,

> Will chose for us children
> what seemed to him the best available schools,
> schools being a major influence in our lives.

Averil and I
began at Miss Franklin's,
a Catholic nursery school nearby.

Maimie would ride me there and back
on the plywood seat on the back of her bicycle.

> At three,
> I cried to go to school,
> like Averil, I'm told;
>
> at four,
> I cried, not to. I went.

I still know the Lord's Prayer:

> "Our Father,
> who art in Heaven. . . ."

and I still love candles.

We started to learn French
and the alphabet
in 26 crayoned pictures.

For "Y"
I can still see
a vivid yellow yacht
sailing across blue waters
lost to memory.

After Miss Franklin's
Averil went to Headington School, for girls
("Go to the Headington
of the class," her teachers
must have said.)

I went to the Dragon School, for boys.

We learned.

**Pause, gentle reader
rest your eyes.**

**A new world
looms**

**weaving
a magic carpet
for a boy.**

24. The Dragon School

"Where did you get
that phony Oxford accent?"
said my high school
physics teacher
in Chicago.

"Oxford, sir," I said.

Will chose the Dragon School for me
for my years six through twelve.

The Dragon was an institution
that could have been tailored
to Will's desires.

"We have failed,"

said its founder in 1908,

"unless we have helped the boy
to develop his mind
and his capacities
in his own way

unless we have given him
full scope for all
the imagination and originality

that is in him."

The Dragon was a private
"prep"- - preparatory - - school
preparing us for a "public" school

> like well-known Eton and Harrow
> or a lesser-known school like Shrewsbury
> up near the Welsh border
> where I'd have gone
> if we had stayed in England.

> The Dragon was a boys-only school,
> except for the infrequent
> sister of a pupil,
> or daughter of a teacher.

> Ever since,
> I've been shy
> with members
> of the opposite sex.

One could live at the school,
or commute;

I commuted, first by bus,
and then, when my intense wish was granted

on my Raleigh three-speed bicycle.

Looking back,
it seems to me
that almost all my wishes in life
have come true, so far.

Partly, from parents and friends,
        partly, perhaps, patience;
        partly, by serendipitous arrivals
        of things I had not known I wanted;
        and sheer, dumb, luck.

                        Partly, in truth,
                        by the adjustments
                        we make:

                        what we get
                        turns out to be
                        what we wanted.

                Or needed,
                like the daffodils
                growing from the
                muzzles of guns
                in the Pentagon parking lot.

        We learn.

25. Latin and Greek

The Dragon equipped us for life
partly by teaching the classics:

Latin

        where labels first
        became attached to things
        for much of the English language

mysterious Greek;

math and French

and a rarity, then,
science, once a week.

            We learned.

26. Sports, of Course

The Dragon included sports,
    on its green playing fields
    gently sloping
    down to the willow-shrouded River Cherwell
    that flows into the Thames by Magdalen Bridge
    a short punt ride away.

            The Cher, downstream,
            fed swimming pools:
            "Parson's Pleasure," for men,
            where bathing suits
            were not required
            and "Dame's Delight,"
            where they were expected.

We played cricket, rugby,
soccer, field hockey,

and in the Cher, learned to swim .

One morning in June of 1944
we tumbled from the locker room
soccer boots unlaced

hearing a vast and massive
drone of airplanes overhead:

Dakotas,
three by three by three by three
in a column from horizon to horizon
heading South to France;
paratroops, we guessed,
on D-Day.

In cricket,
the position I played
was "silly mid-off:"

      close enough
      to the batter's weak side
      to catch, sometimes,
      balls he only blocked,
      rather than hit.

            You had to be silly
            to play that close,
            I guess.

            It was only later
            that I realized
            that I needed to be that close
            to see the ball.

I did well
in the high jump
until Charles Florey

came back from his evacuation to America

with the American technique
of flopping backwards over the bar --

                                        beyond my skill.

I was proudest
when I won the obstacle race

        where agility and speed

        --but also forethought--

        were required.

                The sportsmistress spontaneously
                gave me a cherry
                from the bunch in her hat.

                I sucked on the cherry stone
                all the way home
                on my bike.

                                        Learning.

27. <u>Dragonettes</u>

Of the girls at the Dragon,
I only remember one,
Antonia Packenham, now Fraser,
who beat me in a crawling race
at a birthday party for her brother, Paddy.

Her father handicapped the field:
Antonia, the youngest, was half-way across the lawn;
myself, the swiftest in the trial heat,
with my feet in the flower-bed, had farthest to go.

I thought I'd won, by reaching the opposite flower-bed first
but her father (who was in a better position to judge)
hoisted young Antonia in the air, and cheered her victory.

Antonia is sometimes on the radio
with the most charming voice of anyone I know.

There is nothing nicer, I suspect,
for a girl, than her father's approbation.

I learned.

28. <u>We Learn, At Play</u>

Each morning, in the Dragon playground
we had P.T. - - physical training - - exercises

led by a grizzled survivor of the Boer War, cheerfully.

> We had a prayer and cocoa
> for elevenses, prayerfully.

There was the occasional fight on the playground.

Twice in my life I've fought like a Berserker:
a Viking who battles, oblivious to cost.

> Our family's oral history,
> Will said,
> is that "Stephenson"
> came from "Steffanson,"
> who brought pit ponies

> > - - tiny horses, for the mines - -

> from Norway, when coal and iron
> announced the Industrial Revolution:

> Norway, where the Vikings came from.

My first Berserker fight was on that playground
solid mud, one morning.

We wore our one-piece denim "boiler suits"
        like Churchill's
        instead of short trousers and blazer.

        I was talking with a friend from Ireland
        who became critical of England
        on some trivial point.

        He had the Irish gift of the gab
        and it got my dander up.

                We tusselled;

                I put my leg behind his knee
                and bent him backwards
                toward the mud.

                He sincerely asked me not to,
                but the fighting fit was on me
                and I fear I laid him gently
                in the mud.

                        He and I, grown men now,
                        are good friends, still
                        I'm pleased to say;
                        we housed him
                        when he came to Washington
                        not long ago.

My other Berserker fight was in Canada:
the high school bully picked on a friend of mine

                - - the VP of our two-man chess club - -

past my endurance.

60

Deaf to common sense, I walked up
and punched the bully on the cheek
missing his jaw.

More surprised than hurt
after walking once around
with a blow
he broke my nose.

I felt I was the moral victor.

(Anybody could be,
on those terms.)

Our play included music:
Gilbert and Sullivan operettas, in New Hall;
and we made pipes

- - the kind you play on,
not the kind you smoke - -
starting with a basic, hollow tube;
drilling, by hand,
the holes for finger-tips,
tuning as we went.

Roger Norrington, the future conductor,
made four increasingly elegant pipes
while I made one.

But mine was mine:
decorated with gamboge,
my favorite color
the liquid orange of a tiger
named for the French word for Cambodia
where tigers roamed.

Part of our lives at the Dragon
was sporting, but not play:
some codes of conduct were enforced.
The P.T. instructor taught me
one of the Dragon codes of conduct.

"Who did this?" he asked
of some transgression.

Silence.

"Who did this?" he asked again.

Thinking he really wished to know
I said "Jones did it, sir."

"Fetch me a gym shoe, Stephenson," he said.
It was applied, a posteriori, to me.

I was never caned,
but a gym shoe can smart

I learned.

29. Anybody Could

We had hobbies:

      marbles, or conkers from chestnut trees,
      collecting engine numbers,
      or playing with clockwork trains.

            One of my best friends, Pieder Kuntz,
            a refugee from Vienna
            had an American Monopoly set.

      He died, too soon,
      in a training crash
      in a peace-time Spitfire in the Med.

            Dragons sometimes fly too low.

            Anybody could.

30. Wings

The dragon on our blazers' crest was golden,
wings unfurled:

    my first wings, but not my last.

I played right wing in soccer;
I played "Wing," the Chinese butler,
in a Samuel French mystery
in the community hall in the hamlet of Elgin
when we lived happily in Canada, below Vancouver
    where the forest met the farms.
    Averil had a starring role
    I'm pleased to say.

Later, and happier still,
I met, and fell in love,
and married Connecticut's Cathya Wing
    whom many dots connect:
        beauty and wisdom
        and common sense
        for openers.

All the Wings in the U.S.A., she says
stem either from China, like the butler in my play,

    or from three Wing brothers
    who hungrily (we assume)
    arrived in Sandwich, Mass., in 1632,
        liked what they saw on the menu,
        and stayed.

    Anybody would have.

    Please don't eat the daffodils.

Pause again.

**Bone up,
as it were,**

as people do

preparing for a test.

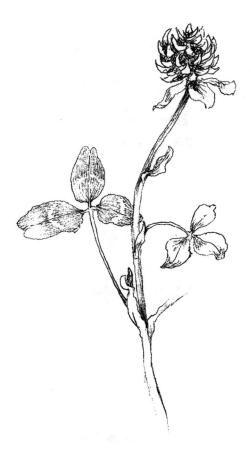

Be lucky.

TESTS

31. <u>Testing . . . .</u>

"Read the top line
on the chart"
they said
at the U.S. Embassy
when I got my visa.

"What chart?"
I asked.

We know
that we connect
the dots of life
as we move through them.

From time to time
we look behind us as we move
          discerning possible patterns in the dots
          like constellations in the stars
          or the linked rubies in the Rubaiyat
          of Omar Khayyam.

Hindsight
lets us see
or imagine
patterns

          some of which are real
          some are not.

We know - - a certain dot - - that Will
was interested in promoting

the development of us children

and children everywhere.

I imagine
as I look back
that, trained psychologist as he was,
he may have guessed that my eyesight was poor.

It was indeed:
I remember at a bus-stop
mentally congratulating
a friend
on his very sharp vision:
he could tell, like Natty Bumpo,
the number on a bus
much farther off
than I could.

A psychologist might be interested, I reason,
in whether a person with a shortfall
in some area, like vision,

would, to compensate,
grow in some other area,
such as the ability to guess
from other clues.

I remember, in Greek class,
how delightful it was
to move to a seat in the front row
near the blackboard
        and to start to enjoy the language
        - - not that I could see each letter

but I could see the shape
of the words, and remember,
and guess,
when I saw that shape again
in the right context,
what it meant.

                              Half of intelligence
                              is guessing right.

Similarly, in cricket,
playing at silly mid-off,
my reflexes grew quicker
to compensate for my poor vision.

Will might - - or might not - -
have got an inkling
about my eyes
when I, a humdrum scholar in geometry
shot to brief brilliance in that class.

Teaching geometry at the Dragon was "Tubby" Haigh,
wounded in the head by shrapnel, on the Somme.

        His large bald spot revealed the scars.
        Tubby sometimes would himself explode
        and throw whatever he held in his hand
        - - chalk, or an eraser - -
        at a seemingly stupid boy.
        I had better luck:
        Tubby must have seen
        that I was trying
        though I did not understand.

Rather than fling chalk,
he asked me to meet him
at his office
at the end of the afternoon.

Leaning over his shoulder
as he explained,
I could at long last see the problem
and understand the answer.

To everyone's surprise
on the next exam
I was top in the Middle School.

When Will saw my report card
with its red inked "1" for first,
he was visibly excited
and sufficiently curious
to hop on his bicycle
and pedal down Banbury Road
to talk with Tubby.

I thought then that he might
have disbelieved my grade

but it is more likely
that he wanted to find out
how it came about.

Tubby will have told him
of our private lesson, I assume;
would Will have guessed
my need for close-up demonstration?

He did not test, as such, my eyes

      but, as I reassemble the dots
      of a possible past

      indirect evidence
      may have existed.

He offered, once, to bowl to me at cricket.
My bat missed each of the six balls he bowled.

He volunteered my services
to an elderly golfing neighbor
so that I could spot
the flight of his shots.

      The elderly neighbor had to report
      - - not without pique - -
      that I had not been any help at all.
      Each ball he hit
      vanished in the sky
      and then lay in the grass
      indistinguishable, to my eyes,
      until a yard or so away
   from a puff-ball mushroom or a seagull's feather.

Does my imagination soar?
Was my father testing me?
And if so, would I mind?

      "Testing School Children"
      was his first book;
      and no, I wouldn't.

32. Relationships

As a scientist,
Will dealt
in relationships.

In science,
relationships have to be testable.

Tests probe relationships
and may shed insight.
They can be fun
as well as useful.

Will devised tests.

In his London days
he earned a pound a week
            - - helpful, in the '30's - -
plus a measure of local fame
from a feature called "Psychojigs"
in the paper:

small puzzles,
like IQ tests,

but which did not rely
on learned word
or number skills

but which probed,
and taught,
the ability
to see relationships.

In my Dragon days
he would sometimes
try on me
intelligence tests he was preparing.

>After one such test
>he worked through, with me,
>the problems I'd got wrong - -
>except for one particular problem
>which he did not explicate.

It was as well that he refrained,
for that test was later given
to all of us at the Dragon School

>- - I did well,
>>given my déjà vu

>>but it would have been awkward
>>if I had got everything right.

>>I was impressed
>>at how well
>>some other Dragons did - -

>>>better than I had done
>>>despite my déjà vu.

It was perhaps part of his method
in relationships with students
to hold something back

>>to leave them room to grow.
>>"Ah, that's the secret,"

I can hear him say
as he failed to share it:

a playfulness, and perhaps a need
to stay ahead.

Will had post-graduate training in relationships:

in London,
he was half of a two-man research project
with Melanie Klein, Freud's pupil
and favorite child psychiatrist,
she analyzing Will
until his move to Oxford halted it.

What was the thrust
of their analysis
I've wondered?

The subject of children
must have come up;

I infer
from what I know
of Will and Freud
and of our family
that part of the direction of their thought
must have been: do not impose authority
if you can avoid it

lead by suggestion
if you can.

Maimie,
icon in our Pantheon,
used gentle authority if needed
for us children
but otherwise led
by love and suggestion
and fun and play.

Years later I asked her
what was her secret
in bringing up children?

"Mostly, I did what Will would do," she said

                    as Michelangelo
                    might have explained
                    that he merely echoed
                    Giotto's perfect circle.

                              Repeatability,
                              as in science.

33. Carnegie Hall

Part of intelligence

- - the envelope Will most wished to push - -

is memory

- - which can be trained - -

part is guessing well

- - which can be trained - -

part is practicing these skills

      and part is listening
          balancing
          judging
          relationships.

               "How do you get
               to Carnegie Hall?"
               said the flutist,
               jumping into the cab.

               "Practice, practice, practice,"
               said the cabbie.

               That's life.

34. Inclusive Testing

Before we sailed for America
in case we should return
Will had me take a test
the "Common Entrance Exam,"

the academic threshold
for any public school

                    Shrewsbury, for me.

Translating the passage from Cicero was hard.

            Will was proud
            that I was the youngest to pass it
            in England, that year

            although the reason was
            because I took it early
            not because I did it very well.

                        The exam was not
                        to keep people out
                        but to let them in.

35. Four Majors

It charmed me
that Will, in the war,
as a Brigadier,
had four Majors
working for him.

They devised tests
for candidates to be officers.

Some of the tests
Will had them test on me
when I was still a schoolboy at the Dragon.

One major, who'd left a leg at Monte Cassino,
took me through a common test of memory
or concentration:
a tray of little objects - -

a whistle, matchbox
spoon and thimble
and the like - -

was shown for half a minute
then covered up. The test
was how many items
you could remember.

The best test
which Will and the Majors invented, or applied
was a test which taught.

It taught tolerance, I believe,

by testing smells.

Take little vials of substance,
some smelling good, some terrible
some golden colored, some gray, some black

sniff each with a blindfold on,
and then without.

A beautiful looking vial
could smell horrid,
and vice versa:

the lesson learned
when the blindfold was lifted
was: do not judge the content
by the color.

War

needs no introduction

I fear.

Mainie.

Flames.

WAR

36. War-time

Will went to war - - World War II - -
we went to school.
Maimie did
the stretching exercises
that you do
in war-time:

adding one fresh egg, she found,
from the weekly household ration
to the packet of dried scrambled eggs from C.A.R.E.
- - Cooperative for American Relief in Europe - -
- - now, for Relief Everywhere - -
transformed a dusty meal for many
into a pile of golden goodness.

Will advised the Royal Air Force.

He was summoned, once,
to a secret base in England's West
for an unannounced purpose
on one night's notice.

His task, he was told on arrival
was to choose a certain number
from the young women there
to be trained as loaders in the R.A.F.:

the ground crews
who loaded the ammunition,
fuel, and lubricant
into the Spitfires and Hurricanes
defending Britain and the West.

"You are the psychologist;
you can decide," he was told
"but do it by this afternoon."

These were ordinary girls
from poorish backgrounds
in the British Isles.

      Having no testing material
      nor time to create it
      he interviewed each, briefly,
      and picked the first ones
      with clean fingernails.

         If they took care of themselves,
         he reasoned
         they would take care of their Spitfires.

Admiring, perhaps, his felicity with ideas
the British Army took him in
as its chief consulting psychologist - -
      in the Royal Army Medical Corps,
      which seemed the closest fit.

Not having gone to Sandhurst
he was sworn in as a private
and promoted, the next day, to Colonel
      with the working rank of Brigadier
      in case he needed to pull rank, they said
         - - like an emergency cord,
            or someone else's leg.

I can still see
the crimson of his shoulder-boards and cap
      the crimson of the British red-coats' tunics
      that Henry VIII prescribed
      so that his soldiers
      would not grow faint at heart
         from seeing bloody wounds - -
            their own, or others'.

37. Burmashave

He was proud to be - - he thought - -
the only Brigadier to come through the war
without a medal

> until he heard there was another
> far up Burma's Irrawaddy River.

> > It was a close thing,
> > Burmashave!

Later, in Will's last decade,
in the network of dots we connect

I found from a bulletin board
at the Department of State

a collector selling medals
including some British service ones
Will was entitled to

> - - not for bravery
> but for being there;

> I sent them to him,
> to, I think,
> his almost unexpressed
> delight.

38. Send for Will

Britain had many shell-shocked soldiers in the war
treated in hospitals and improvised locations.

At one location
recovery rates were very slow.

They sent for Will.

> As his driver
> drove him through the gates
> "First of all" said Will
> "we take down the sign:
> 'Birmingham Lunatic Asylum.'"

War-time India
had the world's largest volunteer army - -
                    five million men.

The British generals were concerned about morale:
there was no enemy to fight.

They sent for Will

> who arrived in New Delhi
> ahead of his kit
> and had to deliver his opening speech
> to generals and men
> wearing trousers, but no belt.

As he got warmed up, gesticulating,
he recounted, his trousers would tend to slip down
                    and he had to grab them
                    and pull them up
                    time and again.

After his talk
the senior general remarked
                "I will say this, Stephenson:
                as your trousers slipped down
                the morale of the men went up
                - - and vice versa!"

Flying over India's Deccan Desert
in a Harvard Trainer
Will, the passenger, sensed something wrong.
"Isn't New Delhi that way?" he inquired.

                "Trust your instruments"
                said the pilot.

                "Trust the sun"
                said Will.

Sure enough, the compass was awry.

                On returning to Oxford
                Averil played the piano for him.

                        "Two years!" he gasped.

                        "Two hundred pounds!"

                        "All she can play
                        is 'God Save the King' - -

                                and I don't believe
                                in either one of them!"

39. The Home Front

                    Meanwhile,
                    Maimie held the home front
                    like Horatio at the bridge.

We had refugees from Europe
and evacuees from London:
a young lady who cried, whenever she could;
an older one, who boiled cabbages, whenever she could;
one from Czechoslovakia who, Maimie later said,
might have been in intelligence
for Resistance movements

because she was visited
by a series of men with European accents
who talked intensely with her for a while

                    and went away.

Tradespeople in Oxford
loved Maimie.

                    Tomato ketchup
                    in the war was rare and precious
                    though not rationed.

                    At our nearby Twinings store
                    as Maimie was filling her order
                    the grocer smiled, dipped under the counter,
                    and volunteered a bottle
                    of Heinz Tomato Ketchup.
                    Alas, outside,
                    as she was hanging
                    her string bag on her bicycle
                    the bottle slipped and shattered
                    on the sidewalk.

Inside again,
shamefacedly to report
the mess to clean up
she was met with a second smile

"- - here, Mrs. Stephenson - -"

and a second bottle of ketchup.

She wore shoes with wooden soles
                if that was all there were;
                we boys wore shirts of "utility" gray
                as that was all there were.

She led the household through the war
                air-raid shelter to air-raid shelter:
                                from the slit trench, not used,
                                dug by Uncle Jack,
                                on leave from the R.A.F.,
to the bunker

                                half-way down the garden
                                with corrugated-iron roof
                                covered by carpet,
                                so's not to reflect the sun or moon

to the deluxe - - it seemed - -
                                Anderson shelter, near the end
                                of the war,
                                in the kitchen, with steel roof
                                doubling as a table
                                with mattress inside
                                where children could fall asleep
                                watching the rosy-fingered glow
                                round the door of the kitchen stove.

She pushed Mariel's pram
back from Port Meadow
    with its concrete pylons
    to stop enemy troop-planes
    from landing

        where Averil and I
        would later learn to ride

as twilight fell,
late one afternoon

and Averil and I were tiring.

"Look," she said
"it isn't far
the moon is following us home,"

        and indeed
        the full golden moon
        stayed level with us
        as ranks of leafless trees
        passed from ahead of us to behind
        as we moved up the gentle slope
        of Davenant Road to home.

40. Coventry

North Oxford,
where we lived,
was lucky in the war.

Cowley, south of Oxford,
where they made the Merlin engines
for Spitfires and P-51's,
was badly bombed three times.

It is odd, what one recalls:
I remember the "ack – ack" - -
the anti-aircraft guns - -
better than the bombs.

A Messerschmitt 109 fighter crash-landed safely
by the Woodstock roundabout
half a mile away;
we all walked over to see.

Its color scheme was vivid,
to a schoolboy's eye: I recollect
crisp, brown-green-black camouflage
bright black and white crosses
sky-blue underneath.

Sound lingers in the memory, too.

As I puttered by the irises in the garden
one spring afternoon
two planes thundered overhead at almost
tree-top height
a Messerschmitt 109,
and hard on its heels, a Spitfire
roaring off towards the open fields to the West
for the Messerschmitt's death
where people on the ground
would not be hurt.

But we understood, also,
that a plane
could waggle its wings
to surrender
and be allowed to land
      as I waggled my wings
      and surrendered
      after I met
      Cathya Wing.

After a raid on a German city
Hitler announced they'd bomb
a beautiful English city in revenge.

    People in Oxford were concerned
    believing Oxford handsome.

    Later, one night, we heard the air raid sirens
        (for years, the crescendos of a warbling siren,
        the signal of an "Air Raid Alert,"
        would still raise the hackles on my scalp.
        "Man and beast," said our zoologist friend
        "that's fear.")

    After the steady "All Clear"
    of the sirens sounded,
    Maimie took us out in the garden
    from where we could see,
    to the North, the red glow in the sky
    from burning Coventry.

        Hitler was saving Oxford,
        was the rumor we heard later
        for his post-war English residence.

    They probably said the same at Cambridge.

41. If Diplomacy Fails

War is what can happen
if diplomacy fails.

> To boys, as I was then,
> war is fascinating
> but Will
> was a pacific warrior
> as Averil said.

He told a seminar
in Missouri
of Louis Richardson's "The Statistics of Deadly Quarrels."

> If you reversed the formulae,
> he said
> you would have

> an outbreak of peace.

War is too much

like

a

repetitive

motion

syndrome.

42. Maximization

A "maxim"
can be a statement
that is repeated
or a gun
that repeats itself.

Sir Hiram Maxim
of Maxim machine gun fame
invented the most effective gun
in the Great War:

the exhaust gas of the first shot fired
pulled the next cartridge into place,
cocked, and fired again
and the bodies piled up
until the barrel overheated.

Where shall we look
for peace's answer
to Maxim's gun - -

a self-perpetuating pacifier?

Thought
is a speedier traveler
than light itself
my friend Quinta wrote.

Words
are the ammunition of our thoughts
Will saw:
the ripple of a thought
pulls the next thought into place,
cocks, and fires,

and the rays of thought
sweep the horizon like a Maxim gun

like the rays from the forehead
of the Statue of Liberty

whose message can be peace, not war
life, not death.

Will's achievement
was to freeze the trajectories of ideas in mid-air
so that feelings, thoughts, beliefs
could be studied
with the objectivity
of the physical sciences.

Statistics, the discipline of numbers,
was the key to this:

statistics,
the analysis of raw data
to show the structure,
the framework of things:

to show where items cluster
like girders in a bridge
or raisins in a pudding.

Will was a master statistician:

> he learned it studying physics,
> and again in psychology
> and found the statistics
> were the same in each.

Physical science is called objective
because it can name and measure things,
    and different people
    performing the same operations
    will get the same results:

> things are testable, in a word.

So, Will saw,
one merely had to label thoughts
and deal with them statistically:

> different people could perform
> the same operations
> and get the same results.

Labelling thoughts is easy:
if you can conceive a feeling, belief or thought
I can write it down.

As to what to do next,
thereby hangs a tale

       like the tail
       on the letter "Q".

Peace.

At last!

Joy.

PEACE

43. P, Q and R

> In the period between wars,
> Will studied paths to peace.
> In particular, he studied "Q,"
> as a key to deciphering feelings.

There were said to be
when Will was taking his fellowship in psychology,

> three modes of statistics
> pertinent to the field:
> P, Q, and R methodology.

> P (a time-phased R) and R
> measured traits
> > like IQ
> > dexterity
> > or reading skill
> but Q measured relationships
> among people.

Will said let's turn Q around,
and let people measure
relationships themselves.

> Labeled thoughts
> lay ready at hand
> to be measured by people.

Q is more than methodology - - a philosophy
with "one man, one vote" at its heart - -

> but a system which sees
> that one man can be taller
> or more sensible
> than another.

On any matter of subjective opinion - -
> what makes a good friend, for instance
> or a good car
>
> or how to balance
> protecting the environment
> and promoting jobs

select what Will called a "concourse:"
a universe of statements - - thoughts - -
about the issue, from books, or papers,
or interviews - - or make them up.

Cull from the concourse a "Q-sample:"
a set of statements encompassing all apparent views
approximately balanced in outlook

> so that bias
> does not have to intrude.

> Type the statements - - the thoughts - -
> 25, or 50, or more - -
> on cards
> number them, for reference
>
> and ask the person or people
> whose views you wish to explore
> to sort them - - a "Q-sort" - -
> into, for instance, a normal curve
>
> with a few, strongly held
> "agree with" or "disagree with"
> statements at each end
> rising to more numerous,
> more neutral
> > statements in the middle.

The thoughts on the cards
flutter like pigeons
swirling,
homing

to their roosts
as arrayed by the sorter
who locates himself
in the pattern of meaning
divulged by his sorting.

And what is rare and useful
sometimes happens

a new factor will emerge:
a new idea
not seen before
by tester or testee

as if a mutant thought
arose spontaneously
to help our lives along.

44. Reversing the Polarity

Will's Q-methodology
reversed the polarity
of how one looks at people

turning the tables
like a carousel
going in reverse.

Conventional assessments
in the "R" tradition
line up people on a scale.

Instead, Will said,
let the person determine how he or she felt
about the subject of the scale
instead of being determined upon it
by others.

A simple reversal,
but profound:

do not tie the individual to a scale
like the heroine tied to a railroad track:
have the scales emanate from a central point

- - the mind of each person, in effect - -

like the rays from the forehead
of the Statue of Liberty

as though each mind
was a hook-and-ladder truck
which could determine
its own extension

like Gwen Verdon
in "Damn Yankees"
snapping off a kick
which seems to pause
at its peak
like Nureyev in mid-air.

Promote the primacy
of the person
was what Will said:

people come first.

105

45. Sunshine

Will saw the future of the world
as being led
by people who could understand
what other people felt.

He saw that Q
could make feelings, thoughts, beliefs

transparent
understandable
transferable

usable;

could fit them into Kissinger's triad:

assemble
sort
decide.

He made a matrix
for mankind to add
transparency to ideas.

"Let the sun shine in"
Freud would have said.
"Get a life."

46. The Generation Next

A month before my birth
Will published in "Nature" magazine a letter
with the mathematical description
of Q-methodology.

But he told me
countless times
in the rest of his life

that he discovered "Q"
on the day that I was born.

> He clearly saw the mathematics earlier
> but I can concede
> that he may have seen the implications
> of applying Q to people
> on the day when I was born.

> For I half think he decided
> in an unspoken way
> to apply
> the philosophy of Q
> to his children

> and to the extent
> of his influence
> to the lives of children
> everywhere.

Partly by suggestion,
he made each of us feel
the center of our universe

> let us be the judge
> of all we could

and be granted, if possible, all of our wishes
not immediately, as you spoil a child
but as appropriate.

        I wished for my Raleigh bicycle
        long before it came.

We were not unique.

        "It is a worthy aspiration of most parents
        to do well by their children,
        to give them the best chance in life...." he wrote.
        "Testing School Children," Chapter 1.

        Bring children up
        on this new basis - - Q, not R - -
        Will said

        bring a generation up;

        with luck
        and with sustained support
        the generation next
        will have a strong, sustainable
        sense of self
        the ability to share it
        and the ravenous need to do so:

            to demand of others
            that they be themselves.

47. The Barriers of Dreams

We are all children
of experimental generations
aching for the sky.

Each of us
connects the random dots of life
into a pattern we can bear
fitting our thoughts
into an arch of hope
that will support
the moving target
of reality.

We bear both happiness and pain
and for children early
past the barriers of dreams

along with relief, and pride
and with the need to thank
the pullers and the pushers

there comes a slight blush

for the conspicuousness of being early
into a realm of turbulent peace
where hope and happiness
and sorrow

mingle still.

48. Fear

Words
are the paddles
of our life's canoe.

We express
our dreams
in them,
and they shape
our fears.

Fear is an internal thing
brewed in the pit of the stomach
and the mind

but it surfaces in words.

My favorite car
was the second-hand Porsche Speedster
that a date talked me into.

I'm glad she did.

I wanted to see how fast it would go
but did not want to risk a ticket.

Take a deserted stretch of road
at night, I thought.

North of Washington,
the George Washington Parkway

curves along the Potomac;
no street-lights in the dark.

The Speedster's streamlined headlights
were not over-bright;
the curving parkway was deserted.

As the speedometer hit 88
I noticed something.

"Charles,"
I said to myself,
"the emotion you are experiencing
is fear."

I slowed.

I felt fear in Resurrection City.

In the demonstration culture of the 1960's
the Poor People's Campaign,
started by Martin Luther King, Jr.,
settled in, in plywood and plastic shelters,
along the Reflecting Pool by Lincoln's monument
to press for progress.

That was Resurrection City.

Quakers supplied the food,
some of us helped serve it.

The mud was deep
that Spring in Washington - -
up to the second buckle
of my four-buckle arctic overshoes

which, from sentiment,
I did not clean for years.

Tempers ran short
towards the end
but when the protesters
began to sling
folding chairs
across the mess-tent
it was time to leave.

Still in the 1960's,
I was offered the chance
to go down to Selma for the civil rights march.

My life would have been different
had I gone
in experience and friendships made
but after pausing
- - I was truly flattered - -
I declined.

There was a charge of $75 for the bus
- - a lot in those days - -
my Porsche cost $750, to compare - -
and to pay that much
for the chance to get shot
did not seem a good idea.

Prudence, or fear?

Fear can jump upward
from synapse to synapse
but words can help, too,
talking within ourselves
helping to de-fuse the fear
making it hop

to somewhere else
where it is more affordable
where the capacity to tolerate fear is greater
transferring it to stronger places.

Fear can be rational
and reduced by actions
          which we frame in words.

          Alone, at night, on a dark street
          in a big city, one may have a fear
          of being mugged, for instance.

          The best remedy
          is to avoid such places;
          the next best, they say,
          to leave at home your credit cards
          but to carry enough cash
                    to avoid the anger
                    of a robber foiled.

Speaking of anger,
I never saw Will angry with a child

                    - - he understood
                    what makes a child
                    do this or that.

With adults,
he had the power
by intellectual argument
and being right
usually to prevail, in conversation

                    but I have the sense
                    that lesser mortals
                    may have somewhat
                    feared him for this
                    although perhaps
                    he did not know it.

49. Affection

Affection will move
from place to place
like fear

from synapse to synapse:

growing, joyous, pleasure.

Will and Maimie
like William and Mary of royal fame
gave the capacity to dream.

Will wanted his children to pass it on,
to carry on his work.

He offered to have me do
a Ph.D. in psychology under him
but I went into law.

Law offered many "Law and ..." openings,
I knew; I wanted
to postpone a specialty.

Law school
is post-graduate
reading and writing,
I later said.

Anyway,
some father-son distance
helps.

Pride.

PERCEPTIONS

50. <u>Coincidences</u>

Speaking of psychology,
as Director of the Oxford Institute
of Experimental Psychology

Will performed experiments
which sometimes needed
constructions to be built.
So he had on his staff
a young man called Stanley
with carpentry and other practical skills.

        Stanley's room had the usual tools:
        saws, hammer, brace and bit,
        level and T-square, and the like.

        Some of the tools
        were emblazoned by their maker
        with the corporate name "Stanley"
        but for years, as a child,
        I thought that the tools
        carried the label "Stanley"
because that was the young man's name.

"Your trouble is"
my son Donald told me, in another context
        "you don't believe in coincidence."

I am still not sure
whether Stanley's name
helped in his selection.

        Will was a cagey fellow.

117

51. The Society for Psychical Research

Wearing his experimental
psychologist's hat
Will worked to probe
the borders of the normal.

Always along the borders:
the ends of the bell-shaped curve,
the normal curve, of distribution.

As in economics
the problem is not in production
but in distribution.

The interesting problems in life
lie at the edges of the curve.

In the 1930's,
He helped to found
The British Society for Psychical Research.

Drawn from half-a-dozen disciplines
- - physics, physiology, psychology
and so on - -
its members investigated claims
of mediums, spirit-sightings, and the like.

They always found, Will said,
fraud
or normal things
or events attested to
by just one person.

I myself - - just one person - - would attest
to seeing, a couple of times
something I'd not experienced before
out at the edge of my experience.

Once, in the office
of a lady lawyer I admire

I saw a light effect
nestled in her dark hair
like a bit of shimmering golden cable
or a piece of golden halo
or a glowing bar of solid sunshine
not longer than a child's barrette
not much thicker than a piece of string.

Polarized light, perhaps?
        She sat with her back to the window,
        clouded sun behind;
        but what I saw
        was closer to the intelligence in her brow
        than to the horizon
        of her head.

Another time, I was lunching with a colleague.

I asked about her soccer playing, and this and that;
She talked nineteen to the dozen, I remember.

Afterwards, outside the restaurant
standing in pale Foggy Bottom sun

I saw the clear, strong overlay
in her brown hair
of the same shimmering golden cable

but much more of it,
arranged like the ribs
in the helmet of Pallas Athene.

Polarized light, again, perhaps?
But most of the ribs
were in the shadow
of her hair.

Did I think
she would talk less
inside a helmet?
Or that she should have one,
for soccer?

I tend to say
if something happens once
be skeptical;
if it happens twice,
believe it.

What do the Legal Adviser's office
and Food for Peace
have in common
besides my admiration?

Perhaps, that is what they call an aura,
I later thought.

52. Seeing Red

>   The eye sees, partly,
>   what the mind expects to see.

Color can appear
from black and white:

>   as I worked on Canto 51, just now,
>   I wrote "51-1" on its first page
>   in my thin lead pencil, black on white.

Yet I saw, for a split second
those numbers in red and black

>   rouge et noir

>   like the thin red lines of blue and red
>   which appear on the "alignment" sheet
>   of our Hewlett-Packard color copier.

>   As my eyes lifted upward from my page
>   I noticed, higher up my desk
>   a small book of Sigmund Freud's
>   with its title in scarlet:
>   "Civilization and its Discontents."

From these converging cues
                - - no, not "Q's" - -

my mind saw, briefly, red
                        in "51-1."

                        How come?

If I associate ideas
as Freud suggests
I think of the P-51
America's premier fighter
in World War II
built on the donated plans
of the Spitfire.

And I think that Freud
was not unconcerned
with scarlet letters.

It is not widely known,
but Freud believed
in extra-sensory perception - - ESP.

He was advised not to say so
on his American tour.

Perhaps he merely had reference to
the edges of the normal curve
where sense
fades into "extra," acute, perception.

Somewhere
between knowledge
and a guess
lies intuition.

But Freud
was practical
too.

53. Dreams From Old Vienna

Freud had a dream.

He dreamed it for
people everywhere.

It was not just for one person on a couch
but for an age.

The Great War was over.

(It was not called World War One
until there was a Second.)

More had lost their lives
than in any war before.

The challenge was not just to win
but to prevent.

Freud put his slippers and his spectacles on,
stroked his beard, and went to work.

In 1930, in "Civilization and its Discontents,"
Freud spoke of :

"The horrors
of the recent
World War."

He asked whether
civilization had become
neurotic.

"An analytic dissection
of such neuroses
might lead
to therapeutic recommendations
which could lay claim
to great practical interest."

"The fateful question for the human species
seems to me to be
whether and to what extent their cultural development
will succeed

in mastering the disturbance of their communal life
by the human instinct of aggression ...."

Freud saw sexuality
as part of the problem

but Eros - - love - -
as part of the answer.

Along the way, in the 1920's,
Freud organized a series
of "kitchen" meetings
at his home in Vienna.

Psychoanalysts were included;
    so were political scientists

    - - Harold Lasswell was there - -

    it was a small but yeasty
    intellectual crew.

History has not recorded
this group's discussion in detail
but one can infer
from the ingredients
that the menu
must have included talk
of the demon's brew they saw around them:

        the fear, emotional deprivation,
        neurosis and aggression
        which had paved the way
        to the war they had just survived.

           "What can we do"
           such a group would say
           "so that those who follow us
           need not face such things
           again?"

The members of the group disperse,
go back to whence they came;
schools of psychiatry and politics,
whole educational systems

        are founded and flourish.

Friendships grow.

Lasswell teaches; writes; later advises Washington
in World War II.

He ends up at Yale Law School
teaching the principles of power tolerance
to students like me.

Tolerance is the key
was Lasswell's message
but exercise power
to see that tolerance wins.

                              "Take it easy,"
                              said Studs Terkel
                              "but take it."

Progressive education spreads.

Dr. Spock begins to speak
              - - the pediatrician, not the alien - -

                              first, he says:
                              love the child.

54. The Spread of Dreams

How do these dreams arise?

Cause is like a river: not a solid block of water
coming down like ice, but a composite
of currents, twists and eddies.

History forms itself, like this river

as Heraclitus observed.

But men and women
like Freud and Lasswell

Dr. Spock and Melanie Klein

like children playing in a stream

(water play is the best play)

want to modify
the river's flow.

On the surface of his novels
Kipling wrote of "the Great Game:"
keeping Russia and China
out of India
above Afghanistan, on the roof of the world.

The Great Game clearly, also, though,
refers to how young men - - or women - -
move from following to leading.

Psychoanalysis has the same aim
as the subsurface goal of Kipling's game:

moving the analysands
from following others
to leading themselves:

autonomous,
in David Riesman's phrase.

Freud and friends
do not march alone:
many others also try

to weave the rope of history
away from war:

some whose job it is - -
government officials

some who volunteer:
Quakers, pacifists
atomic scientists
and George Bernard Shaw.

Their quest is common
their great game:

how to moor
visions of amity
and order
in a restless world.

Priests in Babylon tried

temple by temple
ziggurat by ziggurat.

Empires tried.
Masons with successive layers of secrets tried.

Many a true church tries it still
    keeping partly under wraps
    the secrets of success in such a game,
    as mysteries that would dazzle the unshielded eye
    if chanced on all at once.

            For Freud,
            the object was the opposite:
            not to keep secrets in,
            but to let them out,
            to diffuse the dazzle
            for unshielded eyes
            like yours and mine.

                Transparency.

Will had some rules of thumb.
One was: Nature abhors uniqueness.

    "If you see a phenomenon," he would say
    "you can be sure
    that there are others like it
    out there somewhere."

        So I do not conclude
        that Melanie's work
        with my father
        was unique:
        she worked with others
        in my father's generation
        for my own.

As child psychiatrists and psychologists go
I've not met one I didn't like

and sometimes feel that I've been liked by them:

> like my father's colleague, Helen Koch
> of the gentle German accent
> and the University of Chicago
>
> whose wedding present to Cathya and myself
> was not silver or crystal
> but a set of tools, from Marshall Field's:
> - a Disston saw
> - an Estwing hammer
> - a Wilkinson Sword pruner
> - a pair of Crescent pliers
> - a screwdriver with the brand-name
>   Chrome Vanadium.

Brand-names were a sub-field of Will's:
he suggested "Lark" to Studebaker.

I don't recall a Helen I haven't at least partly loved.

> It's no accident
> that Troy ounces
> are still used to measure gold.

Part of Will's legacy to me
and my generation

implied
but unexpressed

was the wish
that we would take
these dreams of his and of Vienna onward.

Suspension.

CONCEPTUAL BRIDGES

55. "Will"

> "Will," to Nietzsche
> meant determination,
> grit, and drive.

"Will," for me
was my father
William Stephenson
a peer of the realm of the mind

> who had determination,
> grit, and drive
> but also

> intelligence
> affection
> a sense of fun
> and the ability to survive:

> turning misfortune into gain:
> luck or skill
> that was Will.

One can see life
as a series of puns
like "Will" for drive
and "Will" for Dad.

A pun is a bridge
between columns of meaning - -

> meaning, which we clothe with words

words,
with nuances like leaves,
clustered around a branch of meaning

luminous, like fireflies in the dusk

radiant
from our lighthouse minds.

Will had a way with words
as well as numbers
            as well as people.

But he also had less usual skills:

    a knack with tools;

    an artist's ability
    to toss off a pencil sketch.

    He was the architect - - and contractor - -
    of their Missouri home;

    he had an ear for music
    and an eye for art.

                I seem to remember
                from Oxford in the seamless past

                that if Maimie was delayed
                by child-care things
                when they were getting ready to go out
                        he would sit down at the piano
                        and play remembered Chopin.

Asked a question,
he would try to help the questioner
find an answer
in the questioner's own mind.

He would probe for principles
which underlay or paralleled a point.

He had a fund of knowledge
and a fund of stories - -
interesting,
partly because
interested in others;

willing to take a position
on an issue.

No relation, he said
to George Stephenson
inventor of the locomotive
but when I saw the sketch of George
in "Lives of British Engineers"
with exactly the same nose as Will

I rushed right to him,
saying, "You have to be related!"

"No," he said:

"Ever since Roman soldiers
camped along Hadrian's Wall
one out of three boys
in Northern England
is born with such a nose!"

Will followed his dreams:

      to the capital, London;
      to Oxford;
      to America

      then, as now
      dream capital of the world

            with an under-fulfilled capacity
            to make dreams come true.

He toiled, with pleasure, in the vineyards of dreams - -
      in advertising, for example,
      in England and America
      with firms like D'Arcy,
      Leo Burnett, and J. Walter Thompson
      and on his own
      supplementing the salary of a professor.

Q, as it happens,
like a focus group with a graduate degree
can help an advertiser
understand what people like, and why.

         Q helps people explore their dreams
         and, in the world of sales,

                find a better product
                or a product, better.

Creativity is mostly a matter
of putting known things together
in a new order.

56. Prometheus

Will Stephenson
the physicist

        knew that people had to mellow
        if the race was to survive the atom bomb.

           If he'd stayed in physics
           the thrust of his Ph.D.

           - - low energy discharges - -

           would have taken him, he said
           toward those working on the bomb.

"Burr!" said Will:

      - - not imitating Aaron Burr,
        who shot his way to fame
        cutting down on Hamilton
        like Billy the Kid

      - - nor the "brrrr!" we say
        when we are cold - -

but "burr,"
    Will said
    like a dentist's smoothing drill
    blurring the harsher edges of our egos.

               "Open wide"
               Freud used to say.
               "Get a Life."

               "Freude," in German,
               means "joy."

Will Stephenson
the psychologist

knew,
      but did not say
      that the only trouble with people
      is people:

                our gardens still
                have room to grow.

          "Employ the Power of Positive Thinking"
          said the famous gardener,
          Norman Vincent Peale.

          "If you don't believe
          in the power of positive thinking"
          said the minister on Martha's Vineyard
          "try thinking negatively for a week!"

Maimie, still a girl
saw Emile Coué
the well-known optimist.

She painted the scenery
for the Armstrong College Players, in Newcastle
who, in response, let her hear their lecture series.

138

Winston Churchill (out of office) spoke;
so did Stravinsky, whose "Rites of Spring"
had caused riots at the Paris Opera;
so did Coué
who taught that if you said, each day:

"Every day
in every way
I am getting
better and better"

you would get better: it would happen.

Prometheus brought fire
to improve the lot of man.

Will brought a tool
to help man mellow:

Q, with its tail - -
like a gaudy bird of paradise

bringing science's bright plumage
to subjectivity's lush green jungle.

Coué made just one point
but made it well:

    looking hard for progress
    makes it more likely to be found;

    failing that, search for a silver lining;

    and if the worst
    comes to the worst
    remember
    it's an ill wind
    that blows nobody
    any good

        - - even if that body
          isn't you.

          These things
          are trite
          but true

                - - that's why
                  they're trite.

57. Kilroy Was Here

"Spear-chuckers," in operatic slang
are the men in the back row
soldiers who carry spears
part of the chorus, in an opera like "Aida."

My Godfather,
one of Will's teachers in psychology
was a spearman
                    Charles Spearman
                    later made Sir Charles
                    for services to science.

He taught young Will

                                        as Freud
                                        taught young Jung.

Each younger man grew up
            up and away

in the way that each new generation
            wants to surpass
            the previous generation

                    - - the world's want, also.

Somewhere, in the long line of lives
from Babylon to Socrates
from Freud to Melanie Klein to Will

not to mention the Orient
or the Opies, keepers of folk-lore
nor all the other parallel lives
for history does not
put all its eggs
into one basket

somewhere
down the chain of history

people
cooperating
conceived the idea
that nations parallel man

that until men tried
to stop gouging men
or women

nations would not try
to stop gouging nations

and that men's greater willingness
to be aggressive, in attack or in defense
might have been needed in primitive times

but might be the bane, now
of a world

where the collective noun
is larger than the tribe

and the need
is not for talents of gold
but for talents of service

to mediate, to resolve
to share and to survive together.

These are talents, it will be noted,
where men hold no special edge

and indeed,
where women, on the average
may be better.

For times have changed

as much as Falstaff's Hal

changed into King Henry, Five.

Kilroy was here:

Le Roi - - the King - - is killed:

we are all now Princes

or Princesses

carrying our spears.

58. Caryatids on the Acropolis

With Harry Truman
spear-carrier for the world
the buck stopped there.

Now it stops with each of us

to the extent we choose
to bear the weight

or, like the caryatids on the Acropolis
choose to get together

the caryatids who, effortlessly,
prop up the lintel of the universe
upon their shapely heads
and graceful necks

with the best posture in the world
and the far-off future in their eyes.

59. "_. . . Make It So._"

Will felt
that we are all
custodians
of the future.

Long ago
Ptolemy saw the earth
as the center of the universe.

Later, Copernicus
saw the sun as the center.

Will said:

"Our sons and daughters
are the center of the universe

let's make it so!"

We are the stars.
Can we live with that?

60. Stellar Creatures

> "Now is this winter of our discontent
> made glorious by the summer sun of York."
> (Shakespeare: Richard III, I)

Each of us is a star
where points of meaning or conjecture
cluster.

If I connect up the dots of life
according to my mood of love or fear or pride

the lines of meaning or conjecture
which surround us all

intersect
for me
near where I stand or sit.

Will was right:
each of us is central
in our world.

Even the structure of language,
looked at hard,
agrees.

Take the sentence

"Each of us is central
in our world."

Lines of force, it seems,
radiate
in all directions from the pronoun "our"

as surely as gravity
or light from a candle-flame
spreads from a central point
in all directions.

Words
are the glorious
summer sun
of sense.

But words are also flickering, burning flame:
lay them side by side, too closely
            and the energy they convey
            can singe a mind
            and drive it into madness,
            like a medieval peasant
            lost in the forest
            in the presence of the great God Pan.

            The international emergency call
            is MAYDAY, from the French
            "m'aidez - - help me."

            For the level below that crisis,
            the call is
            PAN, PAN, PAN.

147

Civilization and its discontents
have been stirred by words
and by the fear of Pan
and now can be allayed, in the same way

for now we understand
the centrality of ourselves

    a centrality that implies
    there will be times
    when we shall need to stand alone
    in love or fear or pride

    but, with luck, may also stand with other stellar creatures
    of the night or day

    whom we may find
    to balance our momentum
    with their own

    like twin, or multiple, stars
    in orbit with each other

    spinning,
    both in company and alone
    at the same time.

        Every girl
        should have a Peter Pan

           and every boy,
           a Wendy.

61. "Go West, Young Man"

When Will was "demobbed"
- - demobilized from the Army - -
he looked around
in search of work.

Most of the professorships he might have sought, were taken.

America beckoned;
he came to the Psychology Department
of the University of Chicago.

He liked the move not only for himself
but also for his daughters Averil and Mariel.

Higher education
at that time, in England,
was much harder to obtain for women.

America was more open.

Two-gun Stephenson, six papers in each holster
would stroll the streets of academe
shooting at the boots of colleagues.

"Pow! Pow!" he would point
two fingers of disapprobation
and explain with a smile
why the other guy should dance.

Then, he'd be off to consult,
to pay for some more ammunition.

Basically, he was a professor
hunting, shooting, fishing with ideas.

Mainie

Wave!

COMMUNICATION

62. <u>The Margins of the Book of Kells</u>

Will took to Chicago
the knowledge
that words empower:

communication
is the path to progress in this life.

Back in England,
when he edited the Manual of Arms
of the British Army
which had not been fully overhauled
since Waterloo
he found some curious instances
of old fact.

There was, for instance,
the delay
between the time
you pulled the gun into position
and when the manual
allowed you to pull the lanyard.

He asked, and asked, the origin of this superfluous pause
and finally found the oldest Master Sergeant in the army.

(You always find what you need
in the last place you look,
for then you look no further

last means last - -
there isn't any more.

151

It is like being injured
on the last ski run
of the afternoon:
in the fading light
the icy patches
behind the moguls
show up less well.
Crash!
That tends to be
the last run
of the afternoon.)

The Master Sergeant told him
that the delay
was to allow the gunners
to withdraw to a safer
                or at least a quieter
                distance

the horses
that pulled the guns into position
at Waterloo.

                Will understood roots:
                "go to the root of things"
                was his belief

                like that American classic "Roots"
                which permitted half a generation
                of Americans to see
                what took place
                in black and white

                and what we are not over yet.

Speaking of words,
I was at one time
a collector of sets:

a complete Kipling

("Do you like Kipling?"
she asked.
"I don't know"
was the response
"I've never kippled.")

On sale, I bought
the complete Oxford English Dictionary.

Not just for sentiment - - my old home town - -
not just for opportunity
it was on sale for the 400th anniversary
of the founding
of the Oxford University Press
and such sales, I reasoned
could not take place often
but partly for use.

I took it off my income tax
or would have
if I'd had the necessary income to set it against.

Carol Channing - -
speaking of income tax - -
we are all travelers
on the road to Canterbury - -
broke into stardom
to my ken
out of Bennington
where my sister Mariel went.

Carol made her debut
in "New Faces of 1952"
                - - along with Eartha Kitt

with her smile "impossibly wide"
                as the Washington Post described it
and her eyes as broad as Bikini Atoll.

She did an entr'acte across the stage
while they changed the set
behind the curtain.
It was a classic moment
of the American stage
                musical stage or flat
                - - it was a long day's journey getting there,
                but worth the voyage.

Carol sang at the convergence
of two great currants
in the American pudding:

                business and art.

"He takes me off his income tax"
                sang Carol
"so when he buys me Cadillacs
the F.B.I. won't watch his movements
he writes me off as capital improvements . . . ."

Then comes the hook:
she stops;
her huge eyelids bat:

"Not yet?"
She backs off
into the wings.

                    Only to reappear
                    long of leg
                    floppy of limb
                    beautiful as ever
                    when the next entr'acte
                        - - a border
                    between two scenes - -
                    is needed.

"Not yet?"

recurs
a couple of times,
as the scenes shift.

There are times
when the border
is more important
than what is contained within:
a fusion container for the arts,

            breeding reactions in the audience:

            integrating reality
            with the words that describe it.

                        The Book of Kells
                        in Dublin
                        is known for its marginalia
                        not for its text.

155

63. The World Turned Upside Down

The Oxford English Dictionary
is famous for its roots

      a marker for years to come
      explaining origins.

      The quest for roots of words runs deep
      into the base of knowledge.

Two great English-speaking countries
the United Kingdom and the U.S.A.
         sharing the word "United" in their names

diverged in 1776
as students of history know

      as children need to diverge
      from parents

      to establish their own identities.

The countries still share common roots,
a common language.

        Webster, it will be recalled,
        put into his dictionary
        American spelling,
        partly just to be different
        from English English.

The British bands at Yorktown
marking Britain's loss, played
"The World Turned Upside Down."

Some reversals are complete
like Q, reversing methods used before.

Some are late:
for my whole life till I was 60
I was running on my father's rails.

But still, I had not seen
how much he would have liked me
to have followed his pattern
while adding substance of my own.

Perhaps King George, in his mad way,
wished the colonies to push off
the way my father wished me on my way
as well as his.

Will understood
both sides of the Atlantic:

America, which gives an individual
room to grow,
alone, if wished;

Europe, which tends to fit
an individual into the whole.

(Maimie's brother Bill,
in Vancouver
had the saying
on his wall:
"As you wander on
through life, brother,
whatever may be your goal
keep your eye upon
the doughnut
and not upon the hole.")

Europe has the older tradition
but America is the newer splinter group
deep under the fingernails of mankind
leading, instead of Chaucer, now
the pilgrimage
      to our modern Canterbury
      talking
      as we ride.

Up to a point
isolation is opportunity:
      people have wings
      as well as roots
      and need the room to fly.

But we have reached the point
where promise lies in mutual help
against our common problems:

                short-sightedness
                poverty
                environmental damage
                population
                and despair.

The "pond"
      as the Brits
      call the Atlantic
is narrower than it used to be
      like the Pacific.

The difference across oceans, Will understood
is partly the traditions:
the base from which you straddle your world
           like the Colossus of Rhodes
           the giant statue

at the edge of the harbor
straddling the entrance
as Stalingrad did for Russia

and the ships sailed
or did not sail
into safe harbor at Rhodes.

The statue held a lantern
like the torch
in the hand
of the Statue of Liberty

lighting the long way home.

Cecil Rhodes
who endowed the Rhodes Scholarships
wanted to bridge the pond
believing that "the white man's burden"
as Kipling transcribed the term
might as well be shared
between all races and all people

(only men, at first).

We name things as we see them
and the name is a handle
to materialize the thought
so that it can be put into action.

"In the beginning
was the Word . . . ."

64. <u>Words are Hammers, Facts are Anvils</u>

"Women
and children
first . . . ."

There is a convention in life
under which men protect
women and children
from the harsher moments of reality.

Men clean up their language,
for example, in mixed company.

Will understood Freud's wisdom:
how there is reassurance
in understanding sexuality
and sometimes, in understating it.

Maybe, for example, in an understated way
the statue of the Colossus of Rhodes
straddling the entrance to the harbor
resembled

by simple role reversal
like Q's reversal

the Earth Mother
between whose legs
the ships of life
sail to be born
or sail to die.

Virginia Woolf
in "Orlando"
a favorite book of Will's
employed gender reversal
as only an artist could.

In an image
as in art
gender is interchangeable.

In reality,
to propagate the species
the he-male, female difference must exist.

In history
we swing hammers to change things
but need anvils still to craft reality on.

The lessons of history can become indelible
like the tattooed number
on a shopkeeper's arm in Georgetown.

The past is hard to change
though perceptions of it can be revised.

Revisionist History.

From some of its lessons
we protect the children
as we revise the future closer to our dreams.

We have a dream.
Will had a dream.

Partly, he dreamed
that we dream in words.

Words are hammers
and facts are anvils.

Will understood the ontology of the matter:

Damn you, anvil!

Take that, word!

65. The Power of Play

> Will was serious
> about substance
> but also knew
> the power of play
> in his own life
>
> and recommended it
> for others.

For the sheer pleasure of it
and also the utility.

Revising the British Army's rifle drill

> he added
> to the soldiers' familiar
> "Present Arms" and so on
>
> freer elements:
> to twirl, and toss, and balance
> their rifles
> to make them intimately familiar
> with their gear

but also to add the elements
of effort, achievement
and the chance of failure
that are the hallmarks
of the games we play.

> If you enjoy
> what you are doing
> he said,
> you will do it better
> and if you lose
> you will not really lose.

In "The Play Theory of Mass Communication"
he said that while the message may be mass

> the key to communication
> is making sure
> that the message
> reaches the individual

>> and that Q could help
>> by showing how.

Not by reciting facts, he said

> - - "communication-pain" - -

but by adding play

> - - "communication-pleasure:" - -

fun, involvement, voluntary association

which would,
along the way,
enhance the chance

>> of "tolerance for others,
>> concern for the poor,
>> interest in suffering,
>> joy in the pleasure of being,
>>
>> and the like, in all of which
>> the self is everywhere involved."

More could be achieved
in international affairs,
he said, with symbols

    - - such as royal visits - -

        whether by a Queen Elizabeth
        a Mrs. Khrushchev
        or a Jaqueline Kennedy - -

    than by a hundred meetings
    of Foreign Ministers.

"From a consideration of subjective play . . .
we reach into existential psychology . . . ."
               he said.

"From a mass society
of really existing individuals
one might indeed
find new forms of society arising.

        "This, however,
        is the author dreaming"

           he said.

               Dreaming for us all.

Dreaming for us all.

Winter, Columbia Missouri.

CONCLUSIONS

66. Everyman

"Remember"
said the disc jockey:
"Your life is unique.
Just like everyone else's."

As a child,
a pastime of mine
as a boy in Oxford
was tossing a ball
against a wall

- - the yellow ochre, stucco
side of our house - -

and catching it on the rebound
again and again and again.

In later, American days,
more than 40 years on,
Will asked me, twice,
did I remember that?

"Of course," I said.

"Didn't you get tired of it?"
"Each throw was different," I replied.

Typically, for me,
I did not ask him
why he asked.

167

It wasn't to make the point
of individual differences - -

that had been my answer - -
and as a statistician
he knew about that.

I believe his question was significant
since he repeated it
("if it happens twice, take heed!").

What did it mean?

I think
- - judging partly
by the way the query influenced me - -

that his question veiled the suggestion that I might spend

more of my remaining time on earth
more profitably
doing new things
than in repetition.
"Branch out!" "Go forward!"

He used to say that
the average American
changed careers - - not just jobs - -
seven times in his life

- - a preposterous number, I thought;
but my life's not over yet.

The psychologists say
that seven, plus or minus two,
is how many things
the mind can hold at once:

seven, like the digits
in our telephone numbers
(the first three of which
are "chunked,"
for easier recall).

But I digress.

As I approached these Cantos' end,
the question of leadership began to grow.

It came to me
with a violent shock
that somehow
without saying so
Will had wanted me
to be a leader.

After the shock wore off
I rationalized:
why not?

Anyone
could be a leader.

After all,

the first play

- - Will loved the thought of play - -

the very first play

in the English language
was "Everyman."

Perhaps I am Everyman.

We all are Everyman.

67. <u>Leadership</u>

Leadership
like the lever
or the wheel
magnifies
the chance of motion.

Or of non-motion,
if exercised to prevent.

In the game of bridge
the lead is the first card played.

In the game of life, the best lead often is
eye contact, and a smile; a friendly word.

Leadership implies the existence of a cause:
a wish to have something happen
or be stopped.

It implies a relationship, existing or sought
with other people:
a wish to change, or to maintain,
behavior or belief.

" - - - I lead my regiments
from behind"
the Duke of Plaza-Toro sang:
" - - - I find it less exciting."

Will led his regiments
- - students and colleagues - -
from in front:
- - - he found it more productive.

Two parts of leadership
are the twins, pretense and hope.

In high school, in Canada,
  we sang about hope,
  with the wings
        with the wings of an angel
  whispering her message of love.

      "We shall overcome"
      we sang by the Reflecting Pool

    and obstacles seem smaller
    when a confident, joyous voice

            (who was called "the Happy Warrior"?)

with reasons

predicts that success will be achieved
despite the problems on the way

      - - poetic pretense,
        one might say.

      Pretense is too harsh a word
            - - but the Latin for "pretend"
      means "to stretch forward" - -
      and leadership includes
      getting us to link hands or minds
      stretching forward across the gap
      between reality and dream.

Leadership can be cynical,
selfish, or perverse:

      one can use fear
      as well as hope
      to try to lead.
      Indeed, avarice,

or any other sin
or pleasure
can serve as lure.

So, a follower needs to be selective.

Do you share the values
being sought?

And will you share responsibility
for the means used to promote them?

Gurus recommend
that you lead, or follow
only in ways
and only toward outcomes
that you are pretty sure
are sound.

"When in doubt,
do nowt"
my Grandma said.

Leadership
involves responsibility
not just for yourself,
but for others

even for just one other:
a followership
can start as a gang of two.

When the need is great enough
when a threshold has been crossed
each of us can be a leader
even if it's merely crying: "Whoa! Enough!"

Leadership involves

both intellect and emotion - - mind and heart.

It uses symbols

like the cross, or the swastika

or Liberty,

the poster lady from the French Revolution,

leading a charge

in décolletage

with a tricolor flag

across a barricade.

Logic is useful
but a leader works with hunches, too

spontaneous, subterranean thoughts,
not fully choate
not fully clothed with words
arising from beneath the surface of the mind
to be run up the flagpole of the critical world

to see if the author, or the audience, salutes.

To lead may mean no more
than taking a stand upon an issue - -

but there can be much pleasure
- - as well as, sometimes, risk - -
in taking a stand upon an issue.

I associate leadership with affection

flowing in both directions - -
from leader to led, and vice versa.

Affection is donated
not compelled:

leadership worth having
is non-violent:

Gandhi would approve
(- - Mohandas Gandhi,
whose autobiography
was sub-titled,
according to the Washington Post:
"Dress for Success.")

Person-to-person leadership

is sometimes merely
boosting another's morale:

seeking out, and sharing good perceptions
works,

as Emile Coué found.

If Maimie wishes you:
"sleep well
sweet dreams
and a joyous morning!"
you know you've been well wished!

Age is not a factor:
Great-grandmother Maimie leads our family
speaking strongly still for fairness

and her judgment

will stretch far, I hope, into the future:
facing a difficult question,
I ask myself, what would Maimie do?

Part of leadership is many other things,
but part is habit:

start with a smile
and that friendly word.

Try it
- - you'll like it - -
and you'll carry on
and keep on carrying on.

Can leadership be taught?
Oddly enough, it can.

How?
Often enough, by example,
as Maimie says she followed Will
though she could do it on her own if need be.

Or, follow the simple directions in this book

starting young
and starting with love
as you value internal security.

Ask yourself: do I want to make a difference?
And if so: what are your strengths?
What would you like them to be?

It is permissible to wander
while your directions form.

Leaders are often made,
         or self-made,
         not just born.

With luck - - we largely make our luck,
         seizing the opportune moment going by - -

you can follow
         the restless questing of your mind,
         using all of its capabilities - -
         its clustering, shimmering thoughts - -

and craft the kind of song
         you choose to sing.

You will find
as you help yourself to life
that the answers to "how" will come easily

         flowing

                  as the night follows the day
                  and the day, the night

                           singing,
                           perchance to dream,
                           under the stars.

NOTES

p. 18: assagai: a slender hardwood spear or light javelin, usually tipped with iron, used by tribes in South Africa (Webster's definition).

p. 18: knobkerry: a short club with a knobbed end used as a missile weapon, especially by Kaffirs (Webster's).

p. 18: boomerang: a curved or angular club used, mainly by the natives of Australia, as a missile weapon, which can be thrown so that its flight will bring it back near the place whence it was thrown (Webster's). Also used in sport, as a toy, (and as a figure of speech).

p. 31: Arthur L. Liman, 1932-1997. At Yale Law School, Art steered me as far as he could through the draft of a Comment (a medium-sized article) for the Yale Law Journal. He later was Chief Counsel to the Commission investigating the uprising at the Attica prison in New York, in 1971, and Chief Counsel in the Iran-Contra hearings, on national television, in 1987.

p. 32: It is interesting to observe how things are named. Compare the naming of Muggleswick - - derived from the descendants of Mocla - - with the fact that the University of Wisconsin's sesquicentennial ice cream flavor, a pun on the school's "alma mater" song, was named "Hail to thee, our Almond Mocha."

p. 32: French Premier Pierre Mendez-France introduced the slogan: "Drink a glass of milk a day."

p. 51: Headmaster C.C. Lynam's words were quoted, first, in "Remarks to the 17th Conference of the Association of Preparatory Schools, 1908," and recently, in "Dragons," Spring 2000, Bardwell Rd, Oxford, OX 2 6SS, England.

p. 56: Dakota airplane: this was the workhorse Douglas DC-3, known in the military as the C-47. My friend Ab Hamilton has pointed out that the only difference was the location of the door: right side for DC-3, left for C-47. The latter configuration would let you hold on with your right hand, if necessary, before you parachuted out.

p. 56: Charles Florey: some children were evacuated, for safety, to the U.S. and Canada during the war. Some children of persons of high profile were included, on the theory that this precluded the child's being captured and held hostage in the event of Nazi invasion of Britain. Florey's father had discovered penicillin.

p. 63: "...conkers:" a dried horse-chestnut, suspended on a string, is swung at, and hit, by the other boy's conker on a string. One conker eventually will shatter, and the survivor is the winner.

p. 63: "the Med." The Mediterranean.

p. 67: The Rubaiyat was translated from the Persian by Edward Fitzgerald.

p. 68: Natty Bumpo was the guide in James Fenimore Cooper's "Leatherstocking Tales."

p. 68: "...the ability to guess from other clues:" e.g., hearing is said to grow more acute, for blind people.

p. 69: - - the Somme: in World War I in 1916, near the Somme River in Northern France, massed infantry, mostly British, after a bombardment, attacked the German lines, being met by massed machine gun and artillery fire. Over the 140 days of the battle, casualties on both sides were, by the lowest estimate, 1,200,000 men killed, wounded, missing, or captured, approximately evenly divided between Allied (British, Commonwealth, and French) and German. About one-third of the casualties would have been fatalities. (The Imperial War Museum, London.).

p. 75: Giotto: according at least to legend, the Italian Renaissance painter Giotto, applying as a young man for a job, was asked to demonstrate his qualifications. He promptly painted a perfect circle, and was hired on the spot.

p. 80: "...do not judge the content by the color" is, of course, also an allusion to the same theme in the famous speech, by the reflecting pool in Washington, DC, of the Rev. Martin Luther King, Jr.

p. 84: Sandhurst: the officers' academy for the British Army, comparable to America's West Point.

p. 86: The five million-strong Indian Army included men from what are now Pakistan, Bangladesh, Sri Lanka and Nepal as well as present-day India.

p. 88: Resistance movements: people in countries occupied by Germany in World War II carried on the struggle by acts of sabotage, by rescuing Allied pilots who had been shot down, etc.

p. 89: The Anderson shelter was named for the government minister responsible. Although it would not withstand a direct hit from a bomb, it would protect its occupants against the fall of rubble if the house collapsed over it.

p. 92: "Our zoologist friend:" Professor Emeritus William Elder, University of Missouri at Columbia, Missouri.

p. 93: Reversing Professor Louis Richardson's (no relation) formulae would appear, however, to involve reversing time. In psychological terms, perhaps this can be done.

p. 106: Secretary of State Henry A. Kissinger met with the combined U.S. Agency for International Development staff while I was with the Office of the General Counsel there, in one of the interior courtyards of the State Department, no auditorium there being big enough. In the course of his address he defined what he called the three intellectual functions: to *assemble* everything relevant; to *sort* this into relevant categories; and then to *decide* what needed to be decided.

p. 107: "Nature" published Will's letter in May, 1935.

p. 108: William Stephenson, "Testing School Children," Longmans, Green and Co., London, 1949, p. 87.

p. 118: The better-known London Society for Psychical Research was a forerunner - - separate from - - the British Society for Psychical Research.

p. 121: Sigmund Freud, "Civilization and its Discontents," New York, NY, W.W. Norton and Company, Inc., 1961, p. 59.

p. 123: Ibid., p. 91.

p. 124: Id. at 92.

p. 154: Permission pending.

p. 163: William Stephenson, "The Play Theory of Mass Communication," University of Chicago Press, Chicago, IL, 1967.

p. 163: Ibid. at p. 56.

p. 164: Id. at 206.

p. 171: This was Semiahmoo High School, White Rock, British Columbia, named after the Semiahmoo, the local Indian tribe. White Rock was, and is, essentially, where the 49th parallel of latitude, the boundary between the U.S. and Canada, hits the Pacific salt water opposite Vancouver Island.

p. 171: "... link hands..." refers to the "Hands Across America" effort in May, 1986, to have a line of people touching, hand to hand, from the Atlantic to the Pacific, "to take a stand against hunger and homelessness in America." There were gaps, but the effort was significant.

p. 172: In North of England and Scottish dialect, "nowt" means "nothing." Used by Will's mother and her family, including, sometimes, myself.

p. 176: "Brownian motion:" the rapid vibratory movement exhibited by microscopic particles suspended in a fluid (Webster's definition).